LAY BACK THE DARKNESS

LAY BACK
THE DARKNESS

POEMS

EDWARD HIRSCH

ALFRED A. KNOPF   NEW YORK   2004

THIS IS A BORZOI BOOK PUBLISHED BY ALFRED A. KNOPF

Copyright © 2003 by Edward Hirsch

Grateful acknowledgment is made to the editors of the following publications where these poems—some of which have been revised—first appeared: *The American Poetry Review:* "The Hades Sonnets," "Two Suitcases of Children's Drawings from Terezin, 1942–1944." *The Antioch Review:* "The Horizontal Line." *DoubleTake:* "Dates." *Five Points:* "The Magic Mirror," "Work Song," "Self-portrait as Eurydice, III," "Under a Wild Green Fig Tree," "The Evanescence." *The Nation:* "Wheeling My Father Through the Alzheimer's Ward." *The New Republic:* "I Am Going to Start Living Like a Mystic." *The New Yorker:* "My Father's Childhood." *The Paris Review* and *Metre* (Prague): "The Desire Manuscripts." *Princeton University Library Chronicle:* "My First Theology Lesson." *Slate:* "Lay Back the Darkness," "Yahrzeit Candle." *TriQuarterly:* "Reading Isaac Babel's Diary on the Lower East Side," "The Widening Sky," under the title "Whitman Leaves the Boardwalk." "The Horizontal Line" was commissioned by Ned Rifkin for the Menil Museum and appeared in the catalogue *Agnes Martin: The Nineties and Beyond* (Menil Museum and University of Texas Press). "The Evanescence" was commissioned by David Breskin for SFMOMA and appeared in the catalogue *Richter 858* (The Shifting Foundation/SFMOMA). "The Asphodel Meadows" is dedicated to Janet Landay.

Special thanks to the John D. and Catherine T. MacArthur Foundation for a MacArthur Fellowship that helped me greatly in the writing of this book. Warm thanks to Deborah Garrison for her insightful help with this collection.

Library of Congress Cataloging-in-Publication Data
Hirsch, Edward.
Lay back the darkness : poems / by Edward Hirsch.—1st ed.
p.   cm.
ISBN 0-375-71002-7
I. Title.
PS3558.164 L39 2003   2002072991

Manufactured in the United States of America
Published March 2003
First paperback edition September 2004

For my father, Kurt Hirsch (1913–2002),

in memoriam,

and my son, Gabriel Hirsch

CONTENTS

1

2

1

I AM GOING TO START LIVING
LIKE A MYSTIC

Today I am pulling on a green wool sweater
and walking across the park in a dusky snowfall.

The trees stand like twenty-seven prophets in a field,
each a station in a pilgrimage—silent, pondering.

Blue flakes of light falling across their bodies
are the ciphers of a secret, an occultation.

I will examine their leaves as pages in a text
and consider the bookish pigeons, students of winter.

I will kneel on the track of a vanquished squirrel
and stare into a blank pond for the figure of Sophia.

I shall begin scouring the sky for signs
as if my whole future were constellated upon it.

I will walk home alone with the deep alone,
a disciple of shadows, in praise of the mysteries.

THE DESIRE MANUSCRIPTS

1. THE CRAVING

(THE ODYSSEY, BOOK TWELVE)

I needed a warning from the goddess
and a group of men to lash me to the mast
hand and foot, so that I could listen
to swelling, sun-scorched, fatal voices
of two Sirens weaving a haunted sound
over the boiling surf, calling me downward
while I twisted with desire in the ropes
and pleaded to be untied, unbound, unleashed.
How willingly I would have given myself up
to that ardor, that drowning blue charm,
while hopeless clouds scudded overhead
and the deaf oarsmen rowed ruthlessly home.
I was saved, I know, but even now, years later,
I crave those voices dreaming in my sleep.

2. THE RAVISHMENT

(*THE ODYSSEY*, BOOK TWELVE)

I listened so the goddess could charm my mind
against the ravishing sunlight, the lord of noon,
and I could stroll through country unharmed
toward the prowling straits of Scylla and Charybdis,

but I was unprepared for the Siren lolling
on a bed in a dirty room above a tavern
where workers guzzled sour red wine
and played their cards late into the night.

It takes only a moment to cruise eternity
who dressed quickly and left, after twenty minutes,
taking my money. I went back to the ship
and the ordinary men pressing for home,

but, love, some part of me has never left
that dark green shore sweetened with clover.

3. WHAT THE GODDESS CAN DO
(THE ODYSSEY, BOOK TEN)

Maybe it was the way she held her head
or her voice, which was too high, or her braids,
which reminded me of a girl I used to know,

but I sat on a tall chair like a god
drinking a bowl of honey mulled with wine
and getting drowsy, counting my good fortune,

so that she could transform me into a pig
squealing for acorns, grunting and bristling
in a sty, snouting the ground with other swine.

Later, our leader convinced her to reverse
the spell, setting our animal bodies free . . .

I have been many things in this life—
a husband, a warrior, a seer—but I cannot forget
what the goddess can do to me, if she desires.

4. THE SENTENCE

(INFERNO, CANTO FIVE)

When you read Canto Five aloud last night
in your naked, singsong, fractured Italian,
my sweet compulsion, my carnal appetite,

I suspected we shall never be forgiven
for devouring each other body and soul,
and someday Minos, a connoisseur of sin,

will snarl himself twice around his tail
to sentence us to life in perpetual motion,
funneling us downward to the second circle

where we will never sleep or rest again
in turbulent air, like other ill-begotten
lovers who embraced passion beyond reason,

and yet I cannot turn from you, my wanton;
our heaven will always be our hell, a swoon.

5. IN THE MOURNING FIELDS

(*THE AENEID*, BOOK SIX)

The world below is starless, stark and deep,
and while you lay beside me, my golden bough,
plunged into the shadowy marsh of sleep,

I read about the infernal realm, and how
a soldier walked forth in the House of Dis
while still alive, breaking an eternal law

by braving death's kingdom, a vast abyss,
the ground sunken in fog—eerie, treacherous—
guarded by a mad beast, three-throated Cerberus.

Tonight I read about us—foundering, hopeless—
in the Mourning Fields and the myrtle grove,
wandering on separate paths, lost in darkness.

It is written that we were consumed by love,
here on earth, a pitiless world above.

6. AFTER ALL THE ORPHIC ENCHANTMENTS

(*METAMORPHOSES*, BOOKS TEN AND ELEVEN)

After all the Orphic enchantments, after all
was said and done, after a second death stunned
and claimed his wife for the fluttering clouds
and phantom forms, the misting lower depths,

after he pleaded with Charon for a second chance
but was dismissed and chased above ground
where he shunned women for a good three years
and notched a life for himself with young men,

a vegetarian priest who recited the passions
of lovers who paid for their transgressions—
the Cerastes, the Propoetides, Pygmalion,
Myrrha and Cinyras, Venus and Adonis—

after everything was closed, completed,
and the costs were tallied, after he sang
for the hyacinths and virgin laurels
and charmed the drooling souls of beasts,

after he enraged the Thracian women who
circled like birds of prey and ripped him
into pieces, as the gods had prophesied,
after his body watered the ground with blood

and currents carried his severed head chanting
downstream with such a spellbinding grief
that trees shed leafy crowns and stones leapt
up and swollen rivers wept in their beds,

I wonder if Orpheus ever decided it was
worth it after all, relinquishing his body
so he could return to the netherworld
which he knew by heart and where, I hope,

he moves with Eurydice on the other side,
a shade still singing amid the other shades,
sometimes walking behind her, sometimes ahead,
and swiveling round to gaze at her forever.

7. THE REGRET

(THE LOST ORPHICS)

If we had never married, if you had never strolled
barefoot through high grass with a poisonous snake
that sent you weeping alone into the underworld

to join the other shades, the fresh new recruits
arriving at all hours at the way station of eternity,
Persephone's insubstantial realm, the House of Death,

and if I, who could entrance the Stygian fog
and convince the god of our ravishing need for
each other, here and now, in the world above,

had never turned back for my limping wife
on a shadowy path out of utter silence,
the void of Avernus, the margins of earth,

then I might not be floating here alone
on a mournful hillside, devoid of shade,
praising young boys beloved by the fates

to the approaching trees, the bright lotus,
lover of pools, and the bittersweet hazel,
the river-haunted willow and the mountain ash,

awaiting my own death, the crazed Furies
who will send my head and my lyre downstream
still singing about us, what might have been.

2

THE WIDENING SKY

I am so small walking on the beach
at night under the widening sky.
The wet sand quickens beneath my feet
and the waves thunder against the shore.

I am moving away from the boardwalk
with its colorful streamers of people
and the hotels with their blinking lights.
The wind sighs for hundreds of miles.

I am disappearing so far into the dark
I have vanished from sight.
I am a tiny seashell
that has secretly drifted ashore

and carries the sound of the ocean
surging through its body.
I am so small now no one can see me.
How can I be filled with such a vast love?

MY FIRST THEOLOGY LESSON

Rumpled and furious, my grandfather's friend
stood up in a bookstore on the North Side
and lamented the lost Jews of Poland

and declared that he felt sorry for God
who had so many problems with Justice
and had become disillusioned and sad

since He wanted to reveal Himself to us
but couldn't find anyone truly worthy
(it was always the wrong time or place

in our deranged and barbaric century)
and so withdrew into His own radiance
and left us a limited mind and body

to contemplate the ghostly absence,
ourselves alone in a divine wilderness.

LAY BACK THE DARKNESS

My father in the night shuffling from room to room
on an obscure mission through the hallway.

Help me, spirits, to penetrate his dream
and ease his restless passage.

Lay back the darkness for a salesman
who could charm everything but the shadows,

an immigrant who stands on the threshold
of a vast night

without his walker or his cane
and cannot remember what he meant to say,

though his right arm is raised, as if in prophecy,
while his left shakes uselessly in warning.

My father in the night shuffling from room to room
is no longer a father or a husband or a son,

but a boy standing on the edge of a forest
listening to the distant cry of wolves,

to wild dogs,
to primitive wingbeats shuddering in the treetops.

READING ISAAC BABEL'S DIARY
ON THE LOWER EAST SIDE

Morning in the subway, morning in the train,
filthy sunlight on the window, the stale smell
of summer air, sweating bodies, rootlessness.

Farewell, dead men, I'm sinking my teeth into life
and crossing the square, holding my notebook
aloft like a prize, a freshly won trophy.

Describe the usual face of an old market,
a sour apple, two peddlers munching cherries,
a young woman in a white hat lifting her skirt

and wading through a nasty puddle, her style,
the century, Spinoza grinding an eyeglass
in his unimaginable shop, Ukrainian Dickens.

He spans the Pale of Settlement with his hands:
everything repeats itself, governments profess
Justice, and everyone—he winks at me—steals.

Outside, a backyard stocked with chickens.
His daughter married a stork, his son emigrated.
Ill-fated Galicia, ill-fated Jews, stubborn, paling.

I'm sinking my teeth into life—farewell, dead men—
and talking to a Russian woman who needs to borrow
some sugar. Sweet anemic tea and two apple tarts.

Accidentally brushing an elbow against her breast.
Conversation in the corner about rising prices,
unbearable costs. The pogrom in Zhitomir:

begun by Poles, then continued by Cossacks.
Forty-five Jews assembled in the open marketplace,
marched into the slaughteryard, butchered.

Their tongues cut out, their cries. Picture
a mother dropping her child from a burning window
and the yardman who caught him, bayoneted.

I leave shaken, but the story repeats itself
further to the East, Jews plundered at Belyov,
their bewilderment, gravestones toppled at Malin,

Pelcha, Boratyn, the remains of a synagogue
in Dubno, a temple in ruin, lamentations
clustered together in the ashes, Brody looted,

all of it as when the Temple was destroyed,
how the prophet cried out—*and we eat dung,
our maidens are ravished, our menfolk killed . . .*

Life flows on—wretched, powerful, immortal—
and voices blur across the century, bodies
crowded into steerage to Liverpool or Glasgow

or New York, Little Galicia of the tenements
from Grand to Houston. Refugees, peddlers,
prayers for the dead in the next building,

a girl who died from terror after the rape,
the pillage, her mother threatened by grief,
her father swaying, familiar doleful chants

from the benches, an eternal lamp burning
on the windowsill, its reflection in glass,
all the mirrors turned to face the wall.

The promise of a township, village, borough
where many Jews go walking arm in arm
late afternoons in mid-July, the Old World

guiding the New to a corner synagogue.
The Sabbath wanes. I've lost my place
in the prayerbook, the songs my grandfather

taught me, the bliss of a *tsaddik*'s face,
a candle stricken with flame. I've found
an ancient people, still singing at dusk.

Then it's night on the avenues, streetlamps,
this unquenchable carnal lust. The train.
The walk back on quiet, deserted streets.

Remember everything. Describe the streets,
the Hebrew grammar unopened on the desk,
the bearded faces of old Jews, young Jews,

the all-night rattle of a typewriter
penetrating the air. Everything changes,
everything repeats itself in time.

YAHRZEIT CANDLE

You've lit a candle on the counter between us,
a twenty-four-hour mantra to your mother's passing
from one realm to another twenty years ago,

distillation of grief, wick of suffering,
remembrance of how, after the stark drama
of her last illness, the tragic final act,

we ushered her out of her suburban home
like a pilgrim and handed her over to darkness,
releasing her spirit to the air, a wing,

and turning back to each other in light
of our fresh role as keepers of the dead,
initiates of sorrow, inheritor of prayers,

Lord, which we recite but cannot believe,
grown children swaying to archaic music
and cupping the losses, our bowl of flame.

THE MAGIC MIRROR

I was standing in front of *The Magic Mirror*
    by Jackson Pollock in the Menil in late September.
        I was looking at a woman looking in the mirror—

abstracted, but with a feathered headdress.
    She was made of oil, granular filler, and glass
        fragments brushstroked across the canvas

in 1941, the year my parents turned fourteen
    and started "dating." The War was on,
        and black storm clouds loomed on the horizon.

I have imagined it all in slow motion—
    their two bodies coming together as one
        body exploding in rage into seeds and rain.

I was standing in front of *The Magic Mirror.*
    I was looking at a woman looking in the mirror.
    I was walking through the skin of the mirror

into the watery burial grounds of childhood.
    I felt the strokes—black, purple, yellow, red—
        raining down upon me, somehow freed

from the canvas—thick-skinned, light-filled—
    and suddenly I was summoning all the wounded
        animals inside me, totems of childhood,

and letting them go one by one—the mockingbird
    of grief, the nasty crow, the long-beaked
        hawk floating past a picture window flooded

with rain, heading for the Northwest Coast.
　　Oh let the wind release me from the past
　　　　wing by wing, bird by bird, ghost by ghost.

I was standing in front of *The Magic Mirror.*
　　I was looking at a woman looking in the mirror.
　　　　I was walking through the skin of the mirror

into the unexpected country of childhood.
　　I watched my body dispersed and reunited
　　　　somewhere else, transformed, transfigured.

WORK SONG

All day I'd been trying to write
about the work song and the rhythmic origin
of poetry, but I couldn't concentrate

because the dog kept barking
at four or five hands from the museum
tearing down the metal carport

and shouting at each other
as they took turns jackhammering
the heavy concrete in our backyard.

I wanted to say something about the pull
and push of an oar, about hammers and anvils,
about sea chanteys for hauling up sail,

but the rambunctious noise filled my head
like a dentist's drill and the jack-
hammers slowly turned our courtyard

into a floating island of white stones:
my wife wanted a fresh green lawn
and a garden with crape myrtles.

I just wanted to hear Huddie Ledbetter
singing his version of "Take This Hammer"
on a tape I ordered from Folkway Records,

though I had to wait until I snaked along
through rush-hour traffic at three p.m.,
picking up our son from school.

I had a splitting headache and a deadline
and a boy who didn't want to hear prison songs
since he was living in his own prison,

but when we got home the hammers had stopped
and the workers were heaving thick stones
from a wheelbarrow, grunting and laughing

and calling to each other in a soft music
that syncopated their bodies in the late sun
and sounded like *Take this hammer—huh!*

so that the two of us started to hum
and sway in tandem, trailing the leader,
our bodies hypnotized, our voices joining in.

WHEELING MY FATHER THROUGH THE ALZHEIMER'S WARD

Here where everyone forgets everything,
including where they are
or what they are fighting to remember,

I can't help recalling the childhood afternoon
that I was bloodied in a baseball game
by a kid who wanted to murder me,

and how my father, who was streetwise
to the world, a former Golden Gloves champ
in the lightweight division in west Chicago,

laced me into a pair of shiny red gloves
and then chalked a ring in our backyard,
shouting encouragement from the corner . . .

My old man taught me to raise my hands
and keep moving, to feint and weave,
to dance on the balls of my feet

and use my shoulders when I punched,
to stutter-step and lean, to jab hard
with my left, and hook with my right.

My father taught me never to be afraid
to fight, while I grunted and pranced
around our patio under the sweating lights,

bounding off the imaginary ropes
to defend myself, tasting my own blood,
shadowboxing an invisible enemy.

MY FATHER'S CHILDHOOD

I used to bring the conductor his lunch pail
on the trolley that circled Mannheim

but I can't recall now if he was my father
or my father's brother who moved to California.

Maybe if he showed me his wounds . . .

Papa guarded French prisoners in the village
where we moved after he was shot down.

He had trouble breathing after the war.

Sometimes he marched them by our house
and sneaked them in for tea. My mother
made him keep his rifle in the hall.

Otto, she said, and he put his gun away.
Selma came from Enkirch, on the Moselle.

My brother Hans had curly red hair
that looked like a burning bush,
but I was the one who stuttered.

The prisoners sang sad French songs
and gave us pieces of chewing gum
because they missed their families.

I always liked those men who lost everything.

My father had a premonition about the Nazis
and he followed his cousins to Chicago.

He was a spotter,
who never liked working in the dry cleaner's.

We lived in an Italian neighborhood
and I had to fight every day
on the way home from school.

I didn't know English at first
and we were refugees with something to prove.

Sometimes I crawled out my bedroom window
to keep the fight going.

I'd say God was a bully.

You know I can't call up one single word
of German, the bastards,

or the name of that village,

but I remember looking out a window
and seeing my mother standing in a garden.

This was before the expulsion.

I wonder if she ever liked cities.

She was barefoot.

Paradise lived under her feet.

DATES

I am walking under the palm trees in Miami,
buying a cluster of dates from an Arab vendor.

I want to taste the sweet, sticky flavor of
childhood again, its feathery leaves and secret pits.

My Aunt Lil served dates to our family
in ceramic bowls. She baked them into pastries.

She said that the first taste of a date
is like a child's finger in your mouth,

the second is like the hushed sound
of a father's evening prayer.

———

The Sufi Master Ibn 'Arabi believed
that God created the palm tree

from the surplus leaven of Adam's clay.
Adam is the origin and archetype

of all human bodies
and the palm, then, is his true sister.

Adam had a sibling rooted to ground
and branching in wind.

*For us, therefore, the palm
is like an aunt on our father's side.*

———

The date palm is as vertical as faith—
Ibn 'Arabi compared it to a true believer—

and knows desire. The ancient rabbis spoke
of a female palm outside Tiberias

which withered on its own
and only yielded fruit when pollinated

by a male palm from Jericho.
It thrives in valleys of lowland heat.

My love has moved to the mountains
and I am sending her a palm branch.

———

There's a victory palm on Hasmonean coins
and Deborah judged her people in the shade

of one as green and fulsome as the Messiah,
a figure, I'm afraid, who does not arrive in time.

The Romans engraved an image
of the captive Judea—*Judea capta*—

sitting in mourning beneath a palm tree,
but I prefer the sturdy angelic palm

I once saw carved on a stone frieze
in a synagogue at Capernaum in Galilee.

———

When my aunt was too weak to chew,
my cousin mashed a date into puree

and fed it to her with a tiny spoon,
a last honeyed remnant of the garden.

Ibn 'Arabi believed that God laid out
an immense earth from one piece of leaven

the size of a sesame seed.
It was nearly too small to see,

but it unfolded into a world
of plains, mountains, deserts, valleys . . .

———

The sixth Imam, Ja'far Sadiq, explained
that when God banished Adam

weeping from Paradise
and sheltering a naked wife

He ordered him to uproot the palm
and expel it from the garden

and so Adam replanted it in Mecca.
Thus is the bitter made sweet again.

All other palms, East and West, descend
from pits of those first Medina dates.

———

My beloved dreamt of a palm tree
buried inside her, and birds singing

canticles of praise day and night.
The birdsong vanished when she woke up

and soon she forgot the enchantment.
All this happened years ago.

But one night when she tasted a date,
she felt a palm spreading its leaves

somewhere inside her
and pure voices rising with wings.

———

Did I say that the vendor sighed
when he handed me the fleshy fruit?

I wanted the cluster to last
but the sweetness dissolved in my mouth,

which is perishable human clay,
while I strolled under a canopy of trees.

We live on this vast earth for such a short while
that we must mourn and celebrate right now.

A palm leaf is shaped like an open hand.
The taste of dates is holy.

3

THE HORIZONTAL LINE

(HOMAGE TO AGNES MARTIN)

It was like a white sail in the early morning

———

It was like a tremulous wind calming itself
After a night on the thunderous sea

———

The exhausted lightning lay down on its side
And slept on a bed of cumulous sheets

———

She came out of the mountains
And surrendered to the expansiveness of a plain

———

She underlined a text in *Isaiah:*
Make level in the desert
A highway for our God
Every valley shall be exalted
And every mountain and hill shall be made low

———

The mountain grew tired of striving upward
And longed to flatten its ragged peaks

———

The nostalgia of a cathedral for the open plain

———

The nostalgia of a soprano for plainsong

———

I know a woman who slept on a cot
And sailed over the abyss on a wooden plank

———

She looked as far as the eye can see
But the eye is a circle—poor pupil—
And the universe curved

———

It was like a pause on the Bridge of Sighs
An instant before the storm
Or the moment afterward

———

My friend listened to Gregorian chants
On the car radio as he raced down
A two-lane highway in southern France

———

I remember riding a bicycle very fast
On a country road where the yellow line
Quivered ever so slightly in the sun

———

The faint tremor in my father's hand
When he signed his name after the stroke

———

The beauty of an imperfection

———

An almost empty canvas turned on its side
A zip that forever changed its mind

———

From its first pointed stroke
To its last brush with meaning
The glow of the line was spiritual

———

How the childlike pencil went for a walk
And came home skipping

———

It was like lying down at dusk to rest
On the cool pavement under the car
After a blistering day in the desert

———

The beaded evanescence of the summer heat

———

The horizon was a glimmering blue band
A luminous streamer in the distance

———

I recited, *Brightness falls from the air*
And the line suddenly whisked me away

———

No chapel is more breathtaking
Than the one that has been retrieved
On the horizon of memory

———

She remembered the stillness of a pool
Before the swimmers entered the water
And the colorful ropes dividing the lanes

———

Each swimmer was a scar in the blue mist

———

Invisible bird,
Whistle me up from the dark on a bright branch

———

It's not the low murmur of your voice
Almost breaking over the phone
But the thin wire of grief
The hum of joy that connects us

―――

Sacred dream of geometry,
Ruler and protractor, temper my anguish,
Untrouble my mind

―――

Heartbeat, steady my hand

―――

Each year she crossed a line
Through the front page of a fresh diary
And vowed to live above the line

―――

She would not line up with others
She would align herself with the simple truth

―――

She erased every line in her notebook but one
Farewell to the aspirations of the vertical
The ecstasies of the diagonal
The suffering cross

―――

Someone left a prayer book open in the rain
And the printed lines blurred
Ink smudged our fingers when we prayed

———

Let every line be its own revelation

———

The line in the painting was surrounded by light
The light in the painting held its breath
On the threshold of a discovery

———

If only she could picture
The boundlessness of God drawing
An invisible thread through the starry spaces

———

If only she could paint
The horizon without limits

———

A horizontal line is a pilgrimage

———

A segment of devotion wrested from time

———

An infinitely gentle mark on a blank page

———

The stripe remains after everything else is gone

———

It is a wisp of praise with a human hand

———

It is singing on a bare canvas

THE EVANESCENCE

(AFTER GERHARD RICHTER, *ABSTRAKTES BILD*, #858)

1

The day was green and abstract
Like looking at a field from a shaking train

With yellow light smudged
And smeared in the distance.

The dark trees blurred in the wind
And the earth was always rushing past.

2

How the windswept beach at dawn
Resembled Abraham's dream:

He carried a small body
Trembling in his arms,

A sweet kid dipped in blood
For a terrible meat-eating God.

3

The morning was still bruised
By the lingering memory of darkness,

But the gulls—the bloodthirsty gulls—
Called us back to the shore.

Walk with me awhile
In the black-and-blue wake of night.

4

The clouds dissolved in the sky
Over the scumbling waves.

A beach littered with debris,
A sky scribbled with erasures,

And a watery sun floating away.
How does anyone ever sleep?

5

I glimpsed a yellow-beaked redbird—
Radiant, luminescent—

Tilting on one wing
And skimming the shoreline

Just as it was getting dark.
Look. I swear I saw it.

6

I dreamt of a German forest
Dissolving into a red sea.

There were insect creatures
Chasing us, there were metallic birds . . .

The sea parted for us, love,
But then it was soaked in blood.

7

I stood at the Memorial Wall at dusk
And pictured the barbed-wire fences.

The air was thick with testimonies
Written in red ink.

I had not witnessed the violence,
But violence remembered me.

8

The world was rushing by so fast
That we felt dizzy studying it.

The day was gray and abstract
Like looking at the sky from a shaking train.

We had brushed against the light,
We had been brushed by evanescence.

TWO SUITCASES OF CHILDREN'S DRAWINGS FROM TEREZIN, 1942–1944

(IN MEMORY OF FRIEDL DICKER-BRANDEIS, VIENNA 1898–AUSCHWITZ 1944)

1. A CHILDREN'S STORY

Two suitcases sat on a forgotten shelf
collecting dust
                    and waited to be remembered

But when the locks were unfastened
the drawings spilled over
                    like a waterfall
and everyone was drenched

2. ARTIST UNKNOWN

A drawing that looked like the heavens
tilting on one wing

————

A yellow star rising over a blue square

————

A paper cut-out with brown paint
of a man hanging

————

A watercolor on shiny paper
of a girl in pigtails standing with a sword

———

Some wavy green lines on wrapping paper

———

An unsigned still life with a jelly jar
filled with meadow flowers

———

A drawing in red pencil of a candlestick

———

A pasted collage on an office form
of a sunny evening in Terezin

3. WHAT SOME OF THE CLASS DREW

Zuzga drew the saddest elephant in Block 4

———

Karel scribbled his name upside down
under a scrawny camel in the desert

———

Liana painted her face on a tin plate

———

Franta sketched a sleepy ballerina
lifting her leg over a wooden practice bar

She called it *Memory of a Dancing Girl*

———

Petr signed his name in the water
that swirled around the deportation train

———

Soňa crayoned starlight in a dark room

———

František outlined his own hand

———

Mir glued an ambulance from the Red Cross
on semiglossy yellow paper

———

Elly drew a thick diagonal line
but the line needed a partner
and could not live on the paper alone

———

Raja penned an angel with braids
coasting like a hawk over the infirmary

———

Olga created *Paradise with Forbidden Fruit*

———

At twelve
Helga was too old for the children's class
and so she illustrated her father's book

God Came to Terezin and Saw That It Was Bad

.

4. CHILDREN'S VOICES SPILLED OUT OF THE SUITCASE

This evening we walked along the street of death
we saw them taking away the dead in a wagon

———

Don't forget about me
deserted house in the ghetto

———

We made pets out of our fleas

———

I couldn't help laughing
when the mustached man with a bald head
checked Mama's head for lice

———

My suffering took a number

It got in line

———

We listed all the things we couldn't do
like jumping around on our beds at night

We called the game *No Skipping*

———

I dreamt my parents got drunk on wine vinegar
and forgot to have me circumcised

———

Somewhere out there in the trees
far away from the barracks
childhood is still waiting for me

———

The moon was like a soldier
with a bandaged head

The bandage was soaking wet

———

The heaviest wheel rolls across our forehead

———

When you cut the veins of the piano
and let the blood flow through the notes
grief had a new name

———

Your eyes were as dark as skullcaps

Your forehead was as heavy as the heavens before it rains

———

Papa was one of the skeletons
harnessed to a funeral cart
carrying bread to the canteen

———

To make me laugh
the man with a long beard
wriggled his eyebrows

———

Hunger drained the last grays from his face

———

The yellow dandelions flew around our heads
like butterflies

———

Butterflies vanished

5. PARABLES

This is a guard with a stick

This is a stick with a heart

This is a heart with a horseshoe

This is a girl flinging the horseshoe
at a guard

———

The boy drew a suitcase on scrap paper

He folded the paper and put it in a suitcase

He left the suitcase open in the rain

———

All night the girl looked out the window
until the window disappeared
and there was no girl

———

The simple son was pulverized
by the back of a rifle

The wise son forgot to ask

———

We disliked the ancient story
of the sacrificial lamb
who wandered into a slaughteryard

and yet no one revised it

———

No one in dormitory L410 remembered
if the Talmud was written
in black letters on white fire
or in white letters on black fire

———

Some people despise the color green
because it is the offspring
of a mixed marriage
between celestial blue and earthly yellow

———

Someone was always shouting at us
in a language we didn't understand

The Tower of Babel had become a pit

———

She painted herself light blue
when she felt like a flute

She painted herself dark blue
when she felt like a cello

She painted herself black and blue
when she was bruised into silence

———

He drew a German shepherd inside a cage
and blackened the cage with a crayon

It was sealed shut
but he could hear the dog barking at night

———

The passive element of the blue in red
could still make her sad

and the purple light sinking to black
echoed a grief that was scarcely human

———

We did not make graven images
we made images from the grave

———

Not even the teacher
who studied at the Bauhaus
could draw the face of God

———

The Rabbi said that Adonai
hides in the Hebrew alphabet

but we didn't know Hebrew
and we didn't believe him

———

Someone wrote in tiny letters in pencil

I don't believe God forgot us

but someone else scrawled in thick letters in pen

I don't believe

God forgot us

6. THE ART TEACHER

Frau Brandeis said that every object tells a story
if you look hard

She said that art supplies perspective
and engraves memories

She said that childhood is genius

and she praised her teachers who believed
in seven axioms

Force   Intensity   Form   Dimension
Character   Composition   Color

She believed in mixing pigments
and drawing from nature

She taught exercises in composition
and breathing

She spoke of positive and negative forms
and the rhythm of geometric shapes
and the musical keyboard of color

Often we drew with charcoal
to the colorful sound of her voice

She said that we are like mortar
or stone in a fresh building

She told us to imagine ourselves
as an open window or a rising staircase
or a bamboo tree growing in bursts

She said something about the emancipated line
and the aspirations of the vertical

She praised the illuminating hand

Light absorbed her

———

It still seemed natural for her
to pass around pencils and paper

She said
        The wisdom lives in the pencil
and the paper remembers everything

———

But no one drew pictures anymore
after the materials ran out

and the art teacher
was deported

7. ART PROJECT

Cut 15,000 pieces of paper into dolls
Each piece of paper represents one child

Now start a bonfire
and burn 14,900 of the paper dolls

Keep 100

8. THE ANGEL OF MERCY

                        did not get up

It did not unleash our thirty thousand wings

———

Smoke from the oncoming trains blackened our faces

———

Fog invaded the camp

The sky was like a blackboard
clouded with erasures

———

The coward moon cowered in the clouds

———

The city spires pretended to be asleep

Stars muffled their lights

———

The sun at night witnessed everything
from a secret place behind the bridge
but it was too frightened to rise

———

All the transports headed east into nothingness

———

Brushes forgot themselves

Pencils expired

———

Someone stuffed the drawings into two suitcases

———

The drawings whispered like secrets in the dark

———

The secrets were a children's story

———

The story waited patiently to be told

———

Two suitcases sat on a forgotten shelf
collecting dust

9. THE INJUNCTION

At the end of the story
the locks were fastened again

The new teacher shut the school
and went home

———

But the waterfall did not stop
and the magic suitcases could not be closed

―――――

The injunction was scribbled in a child's hand

Whoever looks at these drawings
shall stand under the waterfall
                          and remember

10. FAR AWAY

Somewhere a blue horse floats
over a sloping roof

and a kite soars away from its string

UNDER A WILD GREEN FIG TREE

I am going to eat seven pomegranate seeds
and lie down under a wild green fig tree
in a field that has been ploughed three times

because I want to sleep in fertile soil
sinking into dream time, dream space,
and slip past the door to the underworld,

which has been left ajar for questers
and adepts, for reckless night revelers
stumbling into the corridor of ghosts,

so I can wander the subterranean realm
and listen to Persephone's hell songs,
music she could learn only in Hades—

the low, fateful lyrics of death,
the soul's radical return to innocence,
the earth's eternal movement and passage,

our deep human labor to become spirits,
our almost vegetal need to be reborn,
the cycle of loss, myth of regeneration.

THE HADES SONNETS

1. SELF-PORTRAIT AS
PERSEPHONE

I tasted the white poppy of the dead
and broke the prohibition against food
by picking a pomegranate from the orchard

of Hades, devouring the scarlet seed
that cost me everything, including freedom
three months a year, because I deserved

(or thought I needed) my special doom-
ridden, doom-eager fate, my chosen
place amid the Shades, a secret realm,

the instrument of my initiation
into the darker mysteries, a fatal
sentence of desire, the steep alone,

the void, love, which we call Hell,
Death itself, a schooling for the soul.

2. FRANZ MARC'S LOST PAINTING
ORPHEUS WITH THE ANIMALS
(1907-1908)

Picture the Orphic painter walking alone
through the Berlin zoological gardens
in fall, studying each animal unto itself,
according to its nature, its body,

and then coming home to tame the lion,
a ferocious beast beloved by the ancients,
and the innocent stag, and the egret
flying peacefully over Orpheus's head,

before the blood sacrifices of the war
and the ritual European slaughters,
before the twentieth century had begun
and he moved through a grove of black

poplars, sacred to the death goddess,
and discovered the lost entrance to Hades.

3. THE FORGETFULNESS CHAIR

My obstinate, self-absorbed, courageous
father, shuffling across the living room floor
to the determined chair in the far corner,

where my mother covered him with a blanket
and he promptly dozed off and woke up
later without knowing where he'd awakened,

was Peirithoüs slipping into the under-
world through the open gate at Taenarum
to abduct Persephone, the queen of death,

while Hades, the Unseen One, coaxed him
into sitting down on the chair of Lethe,
the stony black seat of Forgetfulness,

where he forgot why he had entered Hell
and never found his way back to the living.

4. THE ASPHODEL MEADOWS

I dreamt that I found our bloodless Shades
moving among the less distinguished dead
in the Asphodel Meadows, a realm of Hades

reserved for those who are neither good
nor evil, for souls without purpose,
and I poured out libations of blood

before I turned in a fury on Minos
and raged about the past we had suffered
together, our quirky moments of grace,

the loved ones, the deaths we had tended,
the work we had made, the desperate charms
we had uttered on behalf of our child,

but the god was indifferent to our terms,
and then I woke with you in my arms.

5. SELF-PORTRAIT AS EURYDICE

How I dreamt about your engulfing arms,
my Orphic secret, my haunting primal chant,
from my place amid the phantom forms

and waited for you to startle the grave
path into the underworld—dank, silent—
where I shivered in the night's embrace

until I heard your fatal cry, your fate-
ful voice rising like a forgotten dream
or a wandering soul calling for light

in eternity's dense fog, an eager song,
and I followed it toward the earth's seam
hoping to breathe again, listening,

until you whirled around, my dark flame,
and then I died for you a second time.

6. SELF-PORTRAIT AS EURYDICE, II

I shivered in the damp cellar of sleep
on a reckless, swollen, rain-soaked night
that I could neither defer nor escape

and woke up to the harsh sound of light-
ning flashing over the stricken houses
and a lone car prowling the street

like a reproach rising from the darkness
or the sudden dream of being saved
by this wounded desire, a madness

who wound through mazes of the damned
and navigated Hell to find me mired
in the last catastrophe I'd suffered,

but then panicked and turned, my beloved,
and left me floundering among the dead.

7. SELF-PORTRAIT AS EURYDICE, III

Some part of me was already dead
to the world, languishing in darkness
by the time, angel, you breasted the void

and coaxed your way into the motherless
infernal realm where I had waited
without knowing it, in mute hopelessness,

and so I rejoiced to feel my blood
stirring again, and to touch your hand,
and to follow you through worm-eaten ground

to the brightly lit air of the beloved,
a country bountiful and sensuous
where we would always be embodied,

but then you faltered—my flesh, my faithless
love—and betrayed me to the emptiness.

8. TO DEMETER

For I was broken open and shattered
like a pomegranate, or a red poppy,
or a wild heart gushing blood,

but, Mother, you could not save me
from the labyrinth I had entered,
the iron exile, the naked country,

where I needed to find—to comprehend—
my own passageway through the maze
of a mythical world I inhabited,

and therefore I stumbled on my fate,
a song of winter and spring, the story-
book celebration of a deep rite,

although I still dream that someday
we will be together again in one body.

9. SELF-PORTRAIT AS HADES
AND PERSEPHONE

Out of the nether regions of nightfall
in a spectral valley, the House of Dis,
out of the smoky river and black tunnel,

I suddenly recognized myself as Hades
devouring the maidenhead, a fresh girl
staring into the yellow eye of narcissus,

an amorous innocent, a wide-eyed pupil
I also recognized as some part of my-
self ravenous to experience Hell,

eager for dark knowledge of the body,
the long night of the descending soul,
the madness beneath the surface of day,

and so I married myself to a cycle
that was demonic, treacherous, immortal.

10. VOYAGE

I dreamt that you slipped a silver coin
under the tongue of my sleeping body
so I could bribe the miser Charon

to ferry me across the river to Tartarus
where I longed to drink from the pool
of Memory, avoiding the three-skulled dog

on the road to the Fortunate Island
in the Black Sea, near the foaming mouth
of the Danube where I could be reborn,

but I was sentenced to the punishment
field along with other tormented spirits
where I vowed to remember the ghostly

and baleful blue undersongs of Hades
and return with them to the waking world.

Edward Hirsch has published five previous books of
poems: *For the Sleepwalkers* (1981), *Wild Gratitude* (1986), which won the
National Book Critics Circle Award, *The Night Parade* (1989), *Earthly
Measures* (1994), and *On Love* (1998). He has also written three prose
books, including *How to Read a Poem and Fall in Love with Poetry* (1999),
a national best-seller, and *The Demon and the Angel: Searching for the Source of
Artistic Inspiration* (2002). A frequent contributor to leading magazines and
periodicals, including *The New Yorker, DoubleTake,* and *The American Poetry
Review,* he also writes the Poet's Choice column for the *Washington Post Book
World.* He has received the Prix de Rome, a Guggenheim Fellowship, an
American Academy of Arts and Letters Award for Literature, and a
MacArthur Fellowship. A professor in the Creative Writing Program at
the University of Houston for seventeen years, he is now President of
the John Simon Guggenheim Memorial Foundation.

A NOTE ON THE TYPE

This book was set in Monotype Dante, a typeface designed
by Giovanni Mardersteig (1892–1977). Conceived as a private
type for the Officina Bodoni in Verona, Italy, Dante was
originally cut only for hand composition by Charles
Malin, the famous Parisian punch cutter, between 1946
and 1952. Its first use was in an edition of Boccaccio's
Trattatello in laude di Dante that appeared in 1954. The
Monotype Corporation's version of Dante followed in
1957. Although modeled on the Aldine type used for Pietro
Cardinal Bembo's treatise *De Aetna* in 1495, Dante is a
thoroughly modern interpretation of the venerable face.

———

COMPOSED BY CREATIVE GRAPHICS, ALLENTOWN, PENNSYLVANIA

PRINTED AND BOUND BY UNITED BOOK PRESS, BALTIMORE, MARYLAND

DESIGNED BY IRIS WEINSTEIN